Archaeology in Northeastern Ontario

Searching for our past

by Thor Conway

Why northeastern Ontario?

Archaeological investigation in north-eastern Ontario has been underway for some time. What do the archaeologists find? Why do they search for traces of the past? This booklet should help to answer these and other questions about archaeology in northeastern Ontario.

There are more than a thousand known archaeological sites in the Northeastern Region of Ontario. These sites contain a wide variety of clues to a lost world — a world often hidden from us by no more than a few inches of soil.

Archaeology is a process that mixes art and science to achieve its purpose. Mystery, romance, and adventure are a part of archaeology. They help to balance the scales, for much of the work is a slow, detailed search for vague hints of past lifeways.

In the broad expanse of lakes and boreal forest that forms the Northeastern Region, there are many attractions for an archaeologist. Firstly, there is the challenge of a large region that holds a complex blend of the currents of prehistory. Northeastern Ontario includes sizeable portions of two of the Great Lakes, James Bay, three major fur trade routes, and a wealth of geographically diverse areas. Our research can take us anywhere from the pine-covered limestone islands of Lake Huron through wild areas like the Missinaibi River system to seldom-visited shores of Lake Superior.

The weathered faces of these northern Indians in their handmade canoes reflect a life-style that has disappeared. Only legends and archaeology can tell us their story.

I am mesmerized by three topics of Ontario archaeology that dominate this region: the nine thousand years of pre-historic Indian sites; the remains of the fur trade era; and the ancient cliff paintings that are found on its lakes and rivers. Each topic leads me into a world of archaeological sites and artifacts, legends and folklore, and lost artistic traditions.

Documenting the long forgotten chronicle of cultural change in the area becomes more interesting each year. There is an incredible story to be eked out of stone age tools and buried villages. Its central theme is the complex adaptation of Ontario's first residents to the northern forests and waterways. In historic times, the story continues with changes brought by Europeans and the fur trade. Even today, we are a part of these cultural changes.

There is an additional dimension to archaeology in northern Ontario. Unlike many areas across the globe, this area has living ties to the past. Local Indian groups are direct descendants of the ancient hunters and fishermen that we study through our digs. The rich native heritage that surrounds us breathes life into our archaeological finds. Oral history, traditional skills, and other cultural knowledge help to interpret more completely prehistoric archaeological remains.

Finally, the joy of discovery brings a duty to preserve this heritage. The conservation and management of archaeological sites as cultural resources is a major part of every regional archaeologist's job. Working in a defined region over a number of years gives an archaeologist the satisfied feeling that the long hours spent in planning are taking effect.

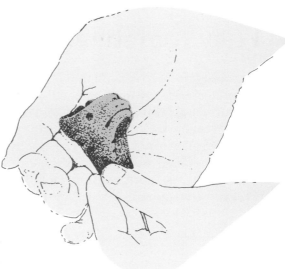

An incredible find. A rare, dog effigy pipe was found while wading in the shallow waters off the Black Thistle site on the St. Mary's River. Such Indian pipes are the last surviving indicators of ancient ceremonies.

There are no sites that are being saved accidentally in these days of rapid resource development and intense recreation. Only careful work preserves a piece of our past for the future.

Another side to preservation is the need to share the archaeological story with the general public. Much of the winter is devoted to writing, making displays, and giving talks to schools and to civic and professional groups.

Careful words may give a general impression of what motivates an archaeologist, but to understand the feeling behind the career, you need to get out on a dig and visit the hidden world of early man.

The region

The map on page one of this booklet shows the area of Ontario included within the Northeastern Region of the Historical Planning and Research Branch of the Ontario Ministry of Culture and Recreation. There are dozens of ways to divide a region into smaller geographical units. For the purpose of this booklet, we found a broad correlation between certain large-scale drainage systems and separate archaeological traditions to be useful. A simplified version of this is depicted by the map on page six. The following geographical areas each have a discrete archaeological pattern that is a mixture of geography, tribal and band core areas, and locally concentrated resources.

A group of Indian rock paintings are hidden at the base of this outcrop in the Temagami area.

AREAS IN THE REGION

1 Saint Marys Corridor
2 North Lake Huron Fringe
3 French River
4 North Lake Huron Interior
5 East Superior
6 Height of Land
7 James Bay Lowlands

— ST. MARY'S CORRIDOR: there is an intense concentration of sites from all time periods along the St. Mary's River. An abundant fishery resulted in dense settlement during the last two thousand years. The area is a natural corridor comparable only to the Straits of Mackinac in Michigan.

— NORTH LAKE HURON FRINGE: there are several pockets of settlement and intense use of local raw materials along the North Channel of Lake Huron. Manitoulin and St. Joseph Islands can be included in this zone, although they demonstrate unique trends in prehistory and geography.

— FRENCH RIVER COUNTRY: the Precambrian Shield levels out in the area around the French River and Lake Nipissing. In the Woodland era, the Indians of this zone were heavily influenced by the Huron. Site distribution patterns and adoption of Huron tools and culture give the zone its identity.

— EASTERN SUPERIOR AREA: a series of Ojibwa bands and their prehistoric ancestors found shelter in the river valleys along Lake Superior's rugged eastern coastline. The archaeology shows much interaction between the small Indian groups.

— NORTH HURON INTERIOR: this drainage area can be subdivided into two archaeologically distinct territories: the greater Temagami area and the Spanish River system.

— JAMES BAY LOWLANDS: little archaeology has been done in this vast area. Because of the harsh climate, strategies for survival differed from those of other areas. There are few spots suitable as population centres.

—HEIGHT OF LAND COUNTRY: the drainage area north of the height of land and below the James Bay lowlands has a concentration of archaeological sites distributed among its lakes and rivers. Distinct groupings have been found around Lake Abitibi and Missinaibi Lake.

An archaeological survey

Much of a government archaeologist's time is devoted to searching out prehistoric Indian campgrounds and fur trade era sites. Archaeological sites are quite easy to find once you know how ancient people lived off the land.

In northern Ontario, many favoured camping spots in areas of predictable food sources were re-used for centuries. A shallow stream or the first rapids of a river offered opportunities to spear sturgeon and runs of suckers in the spring. A temporary fishing camp would be located nearby. On an inland lake, a large sandy beach with dry ground might serve as the main summer village for several Ojibwa or Cree families.

Indian groups regularly occupied territories based on natural geographic divisions of the landscape. For example, the Michipicoten River system from its headwaters at Dog and Wabatongushi Lakes to its entrance into Lake Superior represents a well-defined Ojibwa band territory through time.

In the late summer of 1978 and 1979, I travelled to Dog Lake to begin a search for ancient Ojibwa sites. The map of Dog Lake, on page eight, shows a typical distribution of archaeological sites for a large, interior lake in this region. I located a dozen separate and widely different sites. Previous experience at similar lakes indicates that the twelve recorded sites represent only half of the archaeological potential for a large inland lake.

Dog Lake is a complicated system of inlets, bays, and convoluted arms. Its rocky shoreline varies from low ledges to striking cliffs. The few suitable camping spots used today almost always have evidence of prehistoric use. Except at one large bay, sand beaches are rare on Dog Lake.

ARCHAEOLOGICAL SITES ON DOG LAKE WAWA DISTRICT

A Typical Site Distribution

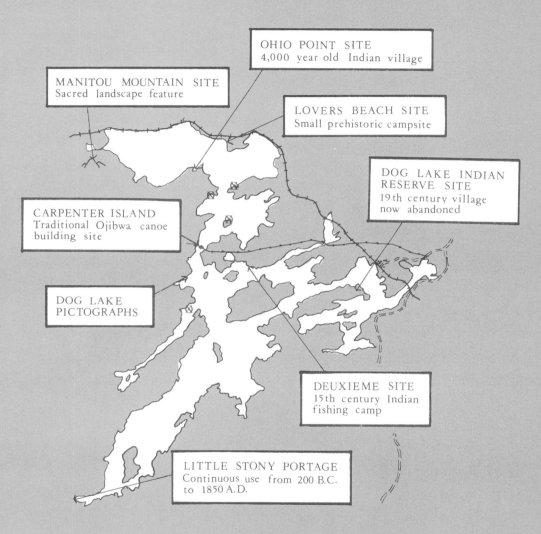

OHIO POINT SITE
4,000 year old Indian village

MANITOU MOUNTAIN SITE
Sacred landscape feature

LOVERS BEACH SITE
Small prehistoric campsite

DOG LAKE INDIAN RESERVE SITE
19th century village now abandoned

CARPENTER ISLAND
Traditional Ojibwa canoe building site

DOG LAKE PICTOGRAPHS

DEUXIEME SITE
15th century Indian fishing camp

LITTLE STONY PORTAGE
Continuous use from 200 B.C. to 1850 A.D.

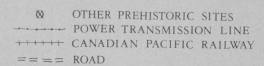

OTHER PREHISTORIC SITES
POWER TRANSMISSION LINE
CANADIAN PACIFIC RAILWAY
ROAD

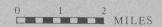

0   1   2   MILES

A report of Indian cliff paintings originally brought us to this lake. The Dog Lake pictograph site is situated on the most prominent cliff in the area. Several moose, thunderbirds, a canoe, strange soaring human figures, and many faint symbols, cover the rock walls of the site.

Prehistoric archaeological sites are found at several headlands and islands. The Deuxieme site was discovered beside a cottage in a sandy cove. There, excavators recorded a fifteenth-century hearth, some flint tools, Indian pottery and — most interestingly — fragments of red ochre. Red ochre is the pigment used for rock paintings. The Deuxieme site is the closest Indian camp to the Dog Lake pictographs that we found.

The earliest remains at Dog Lake are found concentrated on a former shoreline that now lies several feet above the present water level. This once barren sand beach is now covered with dense bush. As we dug test pits along this promising beach, a few flint flakes began to appear in our sifting screens. I decided to open up a small excavation, hoping to discover a prehistoric site.

After a few days of digging slowly with mason's trowels and sifting the soil through screens, our efforts were rewarded. We exposed a concentration of stone tools and debris left by long departed flint knappers (makers of stone tools). The spear points and scraping tools that we unearthed at the Ohio Point site are over four thousand years old. Local fisherman call this area Ohio Point because it is frequently used by fishermen from the "buckeye" state. I wonder if they would ever guess that the fishing has been good for over four thousand years?

Digging involves careful removal of the soil, layer by layer. All artifacts, flakes, and stone lined hearths are measured and plotted on graph paper.

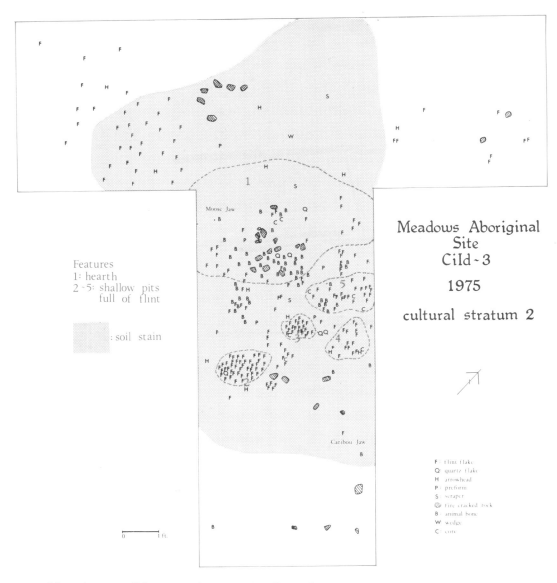

Features
1: hearth
2 - 5: shallow pits
    full of flint

: soil stain

Meadows Aboriginal
Site
CiId-3

1975

cultural stratum 2

F : flint flake
Q : quartz flake
H : arrowhead
P : preform
S : scraper
⊛ : fire cracked rock
B : animal bone
W : wedge
C : core

Moose Jaw

Caribou Jaw

0   1 ft.

After the topsoil is removed, a campsite floor plan is made from field notes. It can be interpreted by a trained archaeologist to reveal the settlement patterns of ancient tool makers.

While Ohio Point provided the earliest evidence of the ancient woodlanders, a small site at the outlet of Dog Lake yielded information about the intervening years of hunting and fishing. Little Stony Portage is a site located beside a series of small rapids. The narrow pathway that connects Dog and Manitouwik Lakes climbs up a rocky knoll, crosses a compact clearing, then descends sharply to the stream. In the level clearing, we dug several excavation units and found a wealth of archaeological remains. Laurel pottery, fired around 200 B.C., appeared in the lowest levels.

As the story unfolded, we were able to trace the use of the area from a stone age level of technology, through the early years of the fur trade, right up to the present. Little Stony Portage is still an attractive resting place, as the top layers of the site show. Our dig at this portage site salvaged remains that were being trampled upon by modern canoeists and wilderness campers.

Word of unusual activity spreads around quickly in small bush communities. During our expeditions to Dog Lake, we met several Indian trappers and guides who helped flesh out the history of the area with their stories and legends. One retired Indian trapper asked if we tried digging on Carpenter Island. During a survey of the shoreline, our crews had noted the small island at the narrows. None had suspected its potential heritage importance. According to the grandfather of this weathered man that stood in front of us, Carpenter Island was a traditional spring campsite used for building bark canoes.

We returned to Carpenter Island, our imaginations fired by the old Indian's stories. It was a changed place. Once regarded as a low, scrubby island barely worthy testing, the site changed before our eyes. We could almost see the piles of birch bark and wooden canoe frames that covered the spot years ago. I pushed a shovel into the thin soil mantle, and immediately a few glass trade beads and shiny flint tools tumbled out of the dark earth. Once again oral history proved to be accurate. We had found an unsuspected site. Carpenter Island is the only ethnographically identified and archaeologically verified Ojibwa canoe building site in Ontario.

A four-thousand-year-old spear-point from the Ohio Point site.

Ojibwa canoe builders at Sault Ste. Marie.

Indian rock paintings

There are over eighty prehistoric rock art sites in northeastern Ontario. These red ochre paintings, or pictographs, occur in several geographical clusters across the region, as shown on the map on the facing page. Each broad group of pictograph sites represents a separate band territory of the Ojibwa. Interestingly, there are unique paintings that occur only in each of these territories.

In the greater Temagami rock art area, bird tracks and a high frequency of abstract symbols can be observed. Moving further west in the region, to the Missinaibi Lake water system, there is a limited distribution of loon paintings along with a recurring strange painting that resembles a sun symbol. Most people are familiar with the predominant figure at the Lake Superior rock art sites: Mishi-peshu, the great horned lynx. But did you ever notice that every painting of Mishi-peshu has a canoe painted beside it?

A loon painting from
Little Missinaibi Lake.

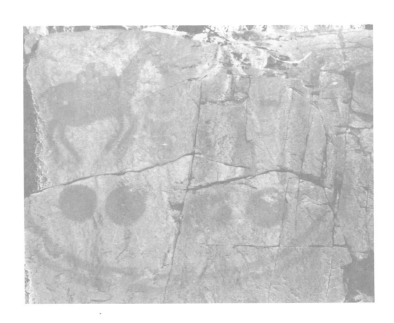

A horse and rider scene at Agawa Bay on Lake Superior is one of the few historic Indian rock paintings ever found in northeastern Ontario.

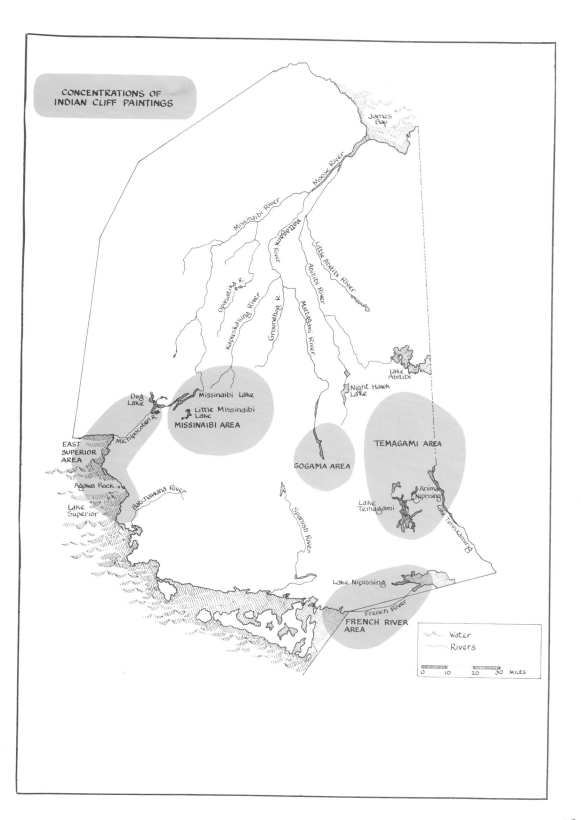

CONCENTRATIONS OF
INDIAN CLIFF PAINTINGS

James Bay

Moose River

Missinaibi River

Mattagami River

Little Abitibi River

Abitibi River

Opasatika R.

Kapuskasing River

Groundhog R.

Mattagami River

Lake Abitibi

Night Hawk Lake

Dog Lake

Missinaibi Lake

Little Missinaibi Lake

MISSINAIBI AREA

Michipicoten R.

EAST SUPERIOR AREA

Agawa Rock →

Batchawana River

Lake Superior

GOGAMA AREA

TEMAGAMI AREA

Anima Nipissing

Lake Temagami

Lake Timiskaming

Spanish River

Lake Nipissing

French River

FRENCH RIVER AREA

Water
Rivers

0   10   20   30   MILES

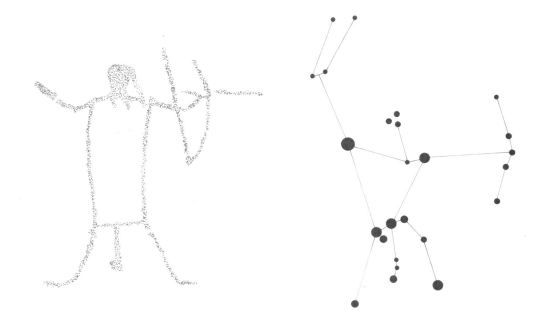

Constellations provide an answer to an ancient riddle

Three years ago rock art researchers Julie and Thor Conway found the secret to understanding some groups of Indian rock paintings. The answer to the often asked question, "What do the paintings mean?" lies above us in the night sky.

A common painting of a man with a bow or raised arms, called THE HUNTER by rock art researchers, is a prehistoric representation of the constellation Orion, (above right). The exact correspondence between the red ochre pictograph and the Orion star group is amazing, (above left).

Further research uncovered numerous groups of THE HUNTER, WOLF, and BEAVER, at sites like the one on Matagamsi Lake, (opposite page). Their positioning and shape strongly suggest the identically placed constellations that we know as Orion, Canis Major, and the Gemini. Indian legends supply the final link in this puzzle. The numerous accounts of Ojibwa folk tale characters who end up in the sky as stars and star groups reinforce this interpretation of the ancient cliff paintings in northern Ontario.

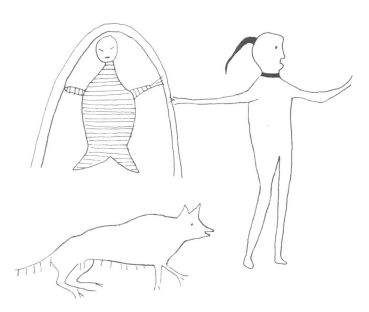

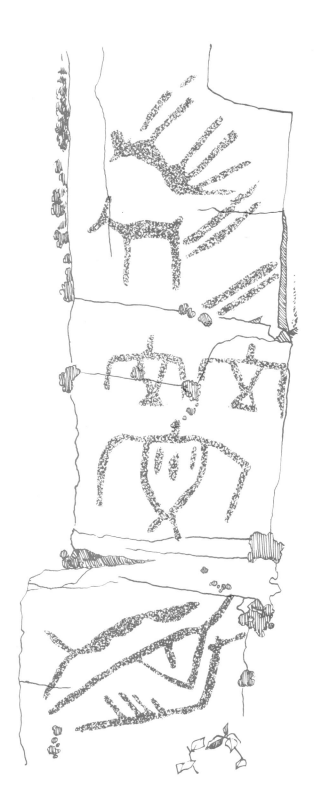

A vertical rock art panel from Wizard Lake near Gogama shows several moose, thunderbirds, and water creatures. A division of the world into land, air, and water creatures appears to be the theme of the ancient artist.

The great horned lynx, snakes, and a canoe at the Agawa pictograph site.

After copying over a thousand separate pictographs, we are starting to unravel a complex puzzle. Just what do they mean? The simplest answer is "many things". All of this art is sacred art, and like religious symbols anywhere, it is highly abstract with several levels of interpretation.

Take the Mishi-peshu pictographs. At one level, the great horned lynx is a familiar figure from Ojibwa folklore — an evil water creature. Numerous tales recall man's encounters with this creature, while other legends tell of conflicts between Mishi-peshu and the thunderbirds. At a more abstract level, the great horned lynx is symbolic of Lake Superior. Like an enraged giant lynx, Lake Superior can quickly become a stormy, fearsome inland sea. In other words, the Mishi-peshu symbol is a cultural abstraction of Lake Superior.

Recently, our research has led us to develop the theory that some groups of pictographs are Indian representations of constellations. The horned man, a wolf, and a beaver pelt occur as a triad at numerous rock art sites across the Canadian Shield. Further research shows that these figures may be identified as the constellations we call Orion, Canis Major, and Gemini (see pages 14 and 15). It is not surprising that unrelated groups of people across the world give an identity to the same star groups. These constellations contain a great number of the brightest stars in the sky.

Here artist and rock art researcher Julie Matey Conway finishes a copy of several canoes at the Agawa pictograph site.

Other work at rock art sites includes preservation efforts to protect them from natural and modern destructive forces. Pictograph sites are a rare and precious heritage. They are the oldest art galleries in Ontario. As storehouses of an ancient knowledge, the cliff paintings offer us a chance to understand another time and a lost society.

Time periods in Ontario

The continuous story of Ontario's past is divided into five periods. Each period overlaps with the previous era.

PALAEO-INDIAN PERIOD

The earliest evidence of human occupation studied so far in northeastern Ontario is concentrated in the Lake Huron basin. Between 9000 B.C. and 7000 B.C., a quartzite knoll on Manitoulin Island was used as stone tool quarry and campsite by late Palaeo-Indian groups. The Sheguiandah site contains large quartzite pre-forms for tools, stone knives, scrapers, and an occasional lance head. Its full story is complicated and long. Similar late Palaeo-Indian sites were discovered in the Killarney area at places like George Lake. Originally, these sites stood on the shorelines of large lakes that were ancestral to the present day Great Lakes. As the glacial ice retreated, the land rose and water levels fell step by step for several thousand years. Now the beach ridges lie well above Lake Huron. The potential for similar sites is evenly spread from Lake Superior's relic shore-lines, now hidden by the dense boreal forest, to the shores of nearly forgotten post-glacial lakes in the Abitibi and Temiskaming districts.

The reliance on quartzite as raw material for larger stone tools continued for eight thousand years.

Digs at Palaeo-Indian sites around the Great Lakes show that the inhabitants of this region had hunted mastodons and caribou. They generally adapted to a tundra-like environment, often living within sight of the slowly retreating glacier. They may have cremated their dead.

We know that early man lived throughout Ontario wherever newly de-glaciated areas appeared. These initial chapters of prehistory are sketchy. To recreate daily life so far in the past, we may always have to supplement the facts with imagination.

PALAEO-INDIAN ARTIFACTS
Palaeo-Indians made large, quartzite artifacts at a site on Manitoulin Island. Most of these items are called preforms. Preforms are carefully flaked stone discs that can be carried away from a quarry and later converted into specific tools.

THE ARCHAIC PERIOD

During the long span of time between 5000 B.C. and 500 B.C. that is covered by the Archaic period, Indians in northern Ontario worked out a successful adaptation to the changing environment. Food resources are cyclical, so they began a repetitive pattern of lakeshore fishing and interior forest living.

The forests north of the Great Lakes are a harsh environment. No single food supply remains constant throughout the seasons, so Indian families moved from fall fowling camps to winter hunting and trapping territories. In the late spring, families united as bands at fishing grounds on major lakes.

This travelling was done within traditional prescribed territories. There is a popular misconception that Indians were unsettled nomads roaming across the whole province. It makes sense to remain in a specific area. You can learn the location and fluctuations of animal herds and fish populations, and you know where to find various raw materials. Even today, our society employs a similar pattern. Modern hunting camps and cottages tend to remain in families for years. Each generation passes along information on the best fishing spots and where to hunt successfully.

The roots of fishing technology began in the Archaic period. Indians didn't have nets then, but they used fish traps, harpoons, and bait fishing. As they developed their fishing skills in extracting food resources from rivers and lakes, they worked from the familiar to the less well-known parts of the environment. The presence of bone harpoons, which work well with species like sturgeon, suckers, and other shallow water spawners, shows that they speared fish in shallow waters. Since Archaic sites have been discovered on islands situated far out from shore in large lakes, we assume that these people had canoes. Some rock carvings in eastern North America, showing numerous people in canoes, are dated to this period. This pictorial evidence may help explain the puzzling presence of stone axes, gouges, and other heavy wood-working tools at Archaic sites surrounding Lakes Huron and Superior. Perhaps there was widespread use of dugout canoes and that these people fished in deeper waters as well as along the shoreline. The more efficient and light weight birch bark canoe, which is so well described in the historic era, may not have been in use during the Archaic period.

As Indian groups settled into well-defined areas around Lake Superior, they discovered local native copper deposits and began to make a wide variety of copper tools. The Archaic period can be thought of as the "great age of copper", because of the diversity and size of its copper artifacts. Large copper axes, socketed spears, pendants, and chisels are often associated with Archaic sites.

The bow and arrow caused another revolutionary change in technology during the long Archaic era. During the later years of this stage in prehistory, small, symmetrical stone points became common at Indian camps. Studies have shown that these flint points are actually arrowheads.

CULTURAL PERIODS	AGE	EVENTS
HISTORIC	A.D. 1600 - PRESENT	*Traditional lifestyles disappeared *The fur trade changed the landscape and settlements *European trade goods replaced stone and ceramic native tools
LATE WOODLAND	A.D. 800 - A.D. 1600	*By the 15th century, the Ojibwa in northeastern Ontario had established strong trade ties with the Huron and Ottawa in southern Ontario *Gill net fishing began *Rock paintings on cliffs spread across the region *Religious ceremonies developed
MIDDLE WOODLAND	400 B.C - A.D. 800	*The start of seine net fishing in shallow water was developed *Pottery was used for the first time
ARCHAIC	5,000 B.C. - 400 B.C.	*Bow and arrow introduced around 1600 B.C. *The first Indians settled at Sault Ste. Marie *Sturgeon and suckers are harpooned and caught in fish traps in local rivers *Copper is discovered as a raw material for tools *Stone axes, gouges and other heavy wood-working tools became common along Lake Superior and Lake Huron
PALAEO- INDIAN	8,000 B.C. - 5,000 B.C.	*Hunting animals such as caribou with spears *Adaptation to a climate cooler than today *Glacial ice still covered part of the region

AREAS OF INTEREST

Fur posts had been established on the Michipicoten River near Wawa and Missinaibi Lake near Chapleau, at La Cloche near Espanola, and Agawa Bay on Lake Superior. Historic Indian sites were located nearby.

380 years

In the Late Woodland, ancestors of the Ojibwa, Cree, and Ottawa developed a specialized adaptation to northern Ontario and its seasonal cycle of food resources. The main sites were concentrated on large rivers and lakes, while campsites can be found almost anywhere.

800 years

The first large villages occurred at places like Sault Ste. Marie, La Cloche, and Lake Superior Provincial Park.

1,200 years

By the middle of the Archaic period, almost every remote lake and river system in northeastern Ontario had some Indian settlements. The spread of people was rapid and thorough. Important Archaic sites occurred near Timmins and Sault Ste. Marie, as well as at Dog Lake, Killarney, Lake Abitibi, and the Temagami area.

3,600 years

A huge stone tool quarry and workshop was started on Manitoulin Island.

3,000 years

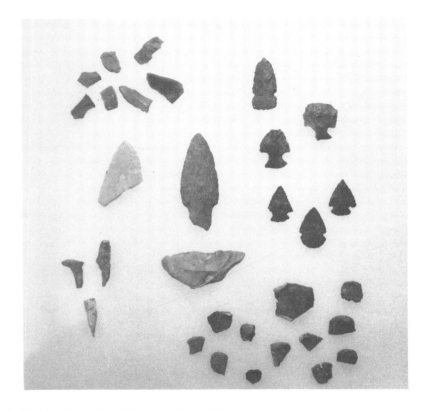

LATE ARCHAIC PERIOD ARTIFACTS

These stone tools represent typical artifacts recovered from small, seasonal Archaic sites. The projectiles (upper right) are dart points and arrowheads. Spear tips (middle left) and flake knives (upper left) are common finds during a dig, but drills (lower left) are much rarer. Scraping tools (lower right) may have been used for a variety of purposes such as woodworking and hide-cleaning.

Previous to the introduction of the bow and arrow, local Indians had used short-shafted spears and a clever wooden spear thrower. This thrower is called an "atlatl", after the Aztec name for it, and is illustrated on this page. The stone tips of the short-shafted spears, also called dart points, are heavier and somewhat larger than true arrowheads. Bow-hunting allows killing at a greater distance from game animals. Most Indian societies quickly developed specialized arrows for use against different species.

A "spear thrower" in use.

EARLY WOODLAND PERIOD

There is a stage of prehistory called Early Woodland that appears in southern Ontario and the lower Great Lakes states. In the upper Great Lakes Region, the Archaic period extends through to the Middle Woodland without there being any Early Woodland cultural developments.

MIDDLE (OR INITIAL) WOODLAND PERIOD

The Middle Woodland period covers the time between 500 B.C. and A.D. 800. During these years, the Indians in northern Ontario adopted pottery vessels as cooking and storage utensils, and they learned to fish with nets.

We recognize two separate, but related, archaeological traditions during the Middle Woodland era in northern Ontario: the Laurel tradition and the La Cloche tradition.

Laurel tradition sites dominate the region. Remains of the Laurel people, who shared the same type of decorated cooking pots and lifestyle, can be found with regional variations from western Quebec to Minnesota.

Large and small Laurel sites, like Whitefish Island, Pumpkin Point, Fort Brady, Metal Toad, and Black Thistle, occur along the St. Mary's River at Sault Ste. Marie. Similar camps have been excavated near Wawa; in Lake Superior Provincial Park; near Timmins; and as far east as Larder Lake near the Quebec border. Material from this period includes distinctive side-notched projectile points, small blade knives, great numbers of scrapers, and some bone harpoons. Laurel pottery is a finely made, thin ware, with numerous rows of decoration. At Sault Ste. Marie, we uncovered several Laurel tradition pots that had red ochre paint on them. Such painted pottery is extremely rare in Ontario.

Whenever we dig into a Laurel site, we find many flat, palm-sized stones with notches at both ends. These were used as weights for nets, and archaeologists believe that the Middle Woodland Indians invented seine fishing. Many Laurel sites are located on points of land suitable for shallow water seining.

Another very interesting artifact appears sporadically only at Middle Woodland Laurel sites in northern Ontario. It is the plummet — a long, finger-like, polished stone that usually has a groove around the top for a suspension line. Plummets may have been used in woodworking like modern plumb bobs. They might also have been used as decorations in magical ceremonies.

A typical plummet with a groove for a suspension line.

Another group of Middle Woodland sites, the archaeological remains of the people known as the La Cloche tradition, occurs along the North Channel of Lake Huron in the La Cloche Mountains from whence they take their name. They lived at the same time as the Laurel people but are distinguished by their distinctive pottery style and stone tools frequently made from local quartzite. Like other Middle Woodland groups, the La Cloche people used stone net weights. It appears that some groups of the La Cloche people maintained strong ties with groups on the Michigan shore of Lake Huron.

Parts of Middle Woodland camps looked like this scene, with fish drying on a rack over a stone lined hearth. Decorated clay pots identical to the one shown here have been excavated throughout the Lake Superior area. A fish net with notched stone weights lies in the foreground.

MIDDLE WOODLAND LAUREL TRADITION ARTIFACTS
Artifacts discovered along the St. Mary's River, between Lake Superior and Lake Huron, provide insights into Middle Woodland lifestyles. Fragments of cooking pots (upper left and top) display several decorative patterns. Laurel tradition projectile points (middle right) and native copper awls (middle left) are commonly found during excavation. The small stone tools, clustered at the lower left, are common flake knives. Flat, notched stones were used as fish net weights.

LATE WOODLAND PERIOD

The last division of the prehistoric era is called the Late, or Terminal, Woodland period. It covers the years between A.D. 800 and A.D. 1600.

The Late Woodland period is the most difficult to summarize as the most is known about it. It is not unusual to find stratified sites from this period, and more have been excavated in the region than have sites from other periods. A stable life-style developed during the Late Woodland period. While decorated pottery styles changed over the course of eight centuries between A.D. 800 and A.D. 1600, the economy and survival strategy remained fairly constant.

The Late Woodland Indians were deep-water fishermen. They repeatedly re-used the same locations for coastal or lakeside summer villages. All along Lake Superior and up to the Michipicoten River, we find linear, or trench-shaped, stone-lined hearths used for drying fish.

By the time of the first contacts with Europeans, the Ottawa, Ojibwa, and Cree had developed an extensive system of trade with the Huron and other southern groups. Huron and other Iroquoian pottery becomes common on the later village sites. Ceremonial clay pipes also appear for the first time in the later years of this period.

Sometimes Indian cooking pots can be partially reconstructed from dozens of excavated sherds.

Dragged lines and tooth impressions from a bone comb decorate this cup-sized pot from the Sand River site in Lake Superior Provincial Park.

INDIAN PIPES FROM NORTHERN ONTARIO
The carefully fired clay pipes to the left of the cord are Iroquoian types found on Ojibwa sites. Such pipes, like trumpet style pipes or ring bowls, came into the Great Lakes by the way of trade. Most of the Iroquoian pipes have polished surfaces. The Ojibwa made less refined clay pipes. A wide variety of designs and shapes occur to the right of the cord. The stone bowl is a local product (lower right), but the catlinite stem (fragments, upper right) was traded from Minnesota.

THE HISTORIC PERIOD

Time travels so quickly that we are often as unfamiliar with our immediate past as we are with the ice age. Historical archaeology encompasses the study of the people of Ontario from A.D. 1600 to the twentieth century. Although there are numerous written records to supplement our appreciation of the last four hundred years, these same records often omit details of common life styles. Historical accounts tend to reflect the biases of the observer, and many of the available archival sources were written by an unrepresentative segment of society. Historical archaeology is capable of uncovering elements of the whole story.

Historic period archaeology in northeastern Ontario is largely the study of three main phenomena: the fur trade; Indian campsites and villages from A.D. 1600 to A.D. 1900; and Canadian settlers.

The various arrowheads and dart points on this page date back to the Archaic period, (lower left), through the Middle Woodland period, (middle), to tiny triangular Late Woodland arrowheads, (upper right).

A bark-covered Indian cabin on the St. Mary's River, about 1880.

Searching for long-forgotten fur trading posts can be an exciting job. After proper preparation in the archives, an archaeologist follows whatever written clues are available to find these sites. Later, the careful methods used at an archaeological excavation will reveal traces of building foundations and concentrations of artifacts. Different activity areas for trade, crafts, and food preparation can also be identified. Slowly, information and patterns can be put together to bring a forgotten historical site to life.

Fur trade sites, like the ruins of Hudson's Bay Company posts at Agawa Bay in Lake Superior Provincial Park, or the famous La Cloche post on the north shore of Lake Huron, preserve the remains of a life-style and economy that shaped northern Canada for over two hundred years. At La Cloche, for instance, we have located the foundations of some thirty buildings, including the trading store, the factor's house, root cellars, labourers' dwellings, a kitchen, privies, and even a small barn.

The thousands of artifacts excavated at posts like La Cloche reveal social patterns and commonplace details of daily life.

Decorated, long-stemmed clay pipes came first from London, later from Glasgow, finally to be replaced by pipes from Montreal suppliers in the third quarter of the nineteenth century. Other humble artifacts (wine bottles, tableware, flintlock rifle parts, even buttons) not only give indications of life at the site but also reflect broader patterns of trade, international relations, and the routes of supply used by the fur trade companies.

Artifacts from French and English traders include a bone comb, (upper, left); gunflints, (right edge); religious items; coins; fancy glass beads; marbles; and parts of clay pipes.

Forgotten

resting

places

These photographs show different historic cemeteries in the Canadian Shield country. The massed graves, fences, and headboards (above) mark a fur traders' cemetery at New Post on the Abitibi River. One ornately carved wooden headboard (lower left) reads, "Sacred To The Memory Of William Luke, Who Died At New Post April 1888, Aged 19 Years". An Ojibwa spirit house, at the Garden River Indian Reserve, near Sault Ste. Marie, lies beneath towering pines. A small opening at the other end was used for leaving food offerings on the grave.

Excavation begins at an undisturbed area behind a junior ranger camp at the La Cloche post site. The large stones are remnants of the cookhouse chimney built by voyageurs.

Quality marks this fine brooch unearthed at the La Cloche Hudson's Bay Company post on Lake Huron.

HISTORIC INDIAN VILLAGES

Although the fur trade has received a lot of attention from various writers, historians, and archaeologists, one portion of the story remains poorly documented. The Indian inhabitants of northern Ontario were the reciprocal half of the fur trade. During the years of rapid cultural and economic change between A.D. 1640 and A.D. 1850, native people changed from a stone age way of life to citizens of a European-oriented country. Recent archaeological field work in northeastern Ontario has helped to unravel the tangled threads of this saga and to weave a fuller picture of the period.

One abandoned Indian village on Lake Superior looks like any other stretch of forest and beach until you kneel in the loose sand and observe artifacts protruding from the ground. The Michipicoten site lies at the mouth of the Michipicoten river near Wawa. It represents two historic Ojibwa summer settlements that are superimposed on top of more deeply-buried prehistoric sites. From a canoe, horizontal dark bands can be seen along the river bank. Each stratum represents a former village that has been covered by wind-blown sand. In a way, the site is a layer-cake of Ojibwa history.

The Michipicoten River causes considerable erosion, and our frequent visits to the site are rewarded by artifact finds that outline the rough draft of an archaeological story. One level of the site is dated to the early fur trade era — a time when first contacts with traders caused abandonment of the old ways. We find portions of the brass trade kettles that replaced the locally-fired clay cooking pots.

An Indian woman from Sugar Island about 1930.

Walking further along the riverbank, I once found a lead musket ball. This item, along with gunflints and broken rifle parts, marks the arrival of firearms. The bow and arrow soon disappeared from use. Today a Great Lakes Indian's handmade arrow is the rarest of museum pieces.

Archaeologists find such artifacts and from them deduce the cultural changes that occurred. But the artifact clues yield further information when pressed. The progression from stone age hunting techniques to firearms produced a dramatic effect on the ecosystem. In the two hundred years between 1700 and 1900, the woodland caribou had been driven to extinction in all but the most remote reaches of northeastern Ontario. Their bones often appear in our digs at prehistoric, and some historic, Indian sites, but after 9000 years of a stable relationship the caribou suddenly disappears. Today only a few isolated herds are the remnants of a once widespread animal. Man tipped the fragile balance with a change of technology.

The stories of the extinct passenger pigeon and the nearly extinct eagles of Ontario are familiar examples of these documented changes between man, his culture, and the land.

Faint clues reveal
a lost fur trader's post

A long lost fur trader's cabin was revealed at La Cloche on Lake Huron when archaeologists stripped away the topsoil and thin layers of sand and gravel. Only the bottom few stones of the fireplaces survived (above and below right) along with stains of floor support beams. Historical records tell of an early post, built in the 1820's, that was destroyed by a flood from a spring ice jam on a nearby creek (artist's conception, upper right). The settlement was later moved to higher ground.

Indians fishing with dip nets in Whitefish Rapids, Sault Ste. Marie.

A typical scene at a historic Indian village.

Underwater archaeology

Towering cliffs on Lake Superior create a dangerous shoreline on the stormy inland sea.

Part of man's past lies underwater. Some archaeological remains, such as shipwrecks on Lake Superior, or lost fur brigade canoes on interior rivers, represent accidental underwater sites. Other submerged sites are the results of deliberate action, like the refuse dumps offshore from old Indian villages.

Underwater archaeology is expensive to do, and it often requires greater artifact conservation facilities than dry land archaeology. Very little underwater archaeology has been attempted in northeastern Ontario, but illegal disturbances of these submerged sites are frequent. As we work with diving clubs, our theme for the next few decades is "save some of our underwater heritage for the future".

Once while diving in the St. Mary's River to observe the effects of a natural gas pipeline trench that cut across the riverbed, I was able to span 4,000 years of time in an instant. A nineteenth-century hotel that had operated on this section of the river had left an underwater accumulation of discarded artifacts. The walls of the pipeline trench glistened with oddly-named painkiller bottles, broken dinnerware, and curiously decorated long-stemmed clay pipes. As I swam along, some forty feet below the modern freighters on the river, I thought of the earlier steamers that had carried these goods through the Great Lakes so far into the continent.

The site lay spread over a considerable area and I made a sketch map of its extent for our records. The opportunity to slice into a riverbed and read its history is rare. After half an hour, my air was almost gone and I turned to swim back up to the riverbank. A bright, oddly-fractured stone that looked out of place on the bottom caught my attention.

Fighting the current, I held onto a rock. With my facemask almost pressed against the river bottom, I let go of my hand-hold, and drifted rapidly toward the curious stone. I marked the spot, grabbed the small rock, and kicked away from the grey-green light of the depths to the silver-coloured glare of the surface.

After leaving the buoyant freedom of the river, I was all too quickly a land creature again, weighed down by tanks, regulators, fins, and mask. I sat on the tailgate of the pickup truck to write down my observations on the underwater dump site. Staring at the river in front of me, I couldn't penetrate the combination of surface glare and choppy waves to see even a few feet into it. I wrote of the blanket of artifacts scattered across the riverbed, and of the effect of the pipeline trench. The bright rock that had caught my attention at the end of the dive turned out to be a four thousand year old spear point. Truly historic waters flowed at my feet.

A shipwreck in the St. Mary's River.

Some important sites

Few people realize how many different types of archaeological sites exist in Ontario. The following sample of actual sites covers a wide variety of Indian and Euro-Canadian settlements ranging in time from the last ice age to almost yesterday. It is hoped that these thumbnail accounts will provide some indication of the breadth of our archaeological heritage.

Whitefish Island once looked like this village on the Michigan shore of the St. Mary's River.

WHITEFISH ISLAND—A LARGE INDIAN VILLAGE IN DOWNTOWN SAULT STE MARIE

The hawthorns were so thick that the only way to move through them was to crawl about on my hands and knees. Some people imagine an archaeologist as a person with his feet firmly planted into the earth. On Whitefish Island, I personified the stereotype with my nose literally skimming the ground. What a relief it was to come to the edge of this long, low island and to stand straight and admire the ever-tumbling Whitefish Rapids of the St. Mary's River.

Located in the middle of the St. Mary's River, near downtown Sault Ste. Marie, Whitefish Island is one of the largest Indian settlements in the upper Great Lakes. This island served as a campsite for seven cultural periods from the Middle Woodland to the post-Confederation historic era. Archaeological remains are concentrated most densely on the south side of the boulder-strewn island, nearest to the rapids. Our excavations, which sampled less than 5% of the total site area, revealed a record of continuous Ojibwa occupation from 200 B.C. to A.D. 1600, with a resettlement of the island in the 1830's. We uncovered thousands of fragments of Indian cooking pots and many other artifacts such as flint tools, bone harpoons, native copper ornaments, ceremonial Indian pipes, spears, and stone knives. The two millenia of occupation are confined to a soil zone only eighteen inches thick.

Any large site with settlements spanning two thousand years is an important site. Whitefish Island is doubly significant. Not only is the site rich in artifacts and other information, but it is also the sole surviving prehistoric Ojibwa village in an area of industrial and commercial development.

Whitefish Island has been protected from disturbance ever since the Canadian shipping canal and boat lock were built through nearby St. Mary's Island. Access is restricted; it is necessary to walk across the top of the lock gates to reach Whitefish Island.

Aside from abundant artifacts, Whitefish Island holds prehistoric hearths full of animal and fish bone. These items give us an accurate look at the change in species distribution through time. The Indians harvested food resources including whitefish, suckers, walleyes, turtles, loons, bald eagles, moose, caribou, otters, black bear, hares, and beaver. Carefully buried dog skeletons and the feet and claws of black bears at this site indicate the antiquity of the secret rites of the dog feast and the northern bear cult.

Whitefish Island was helpful in fully documenting the nature of Ojibwa prehistory for the first time. Enough "foreign" artifacts were uncovered at the digs to identify a thriving trade network between the Huron and Ojibwa.

On the eastern edge of Whitefish Island, we found the archaeological remains of a late nineteenth-century Ojibwa settlement that served as an Indian Reserve for nearly fifty years. Digging into the ground where small cabins once stood, we explored evidence of a transitional Indian society. Arrowheads and bone tools were long gone, replaced by English tableware, glass bottles, metal buttons from Euro-Canadian clothing, coal, cast iron cook stoves, lead net weights, iron harpoons, and many more historic artifacts. This dig was one of the first to be done on an Indian Reserve period site in Ontario. The insight that can be gained from such a recent but poorly documented period of native life in transition enables us to understand the meeting point between two diverse cultures.

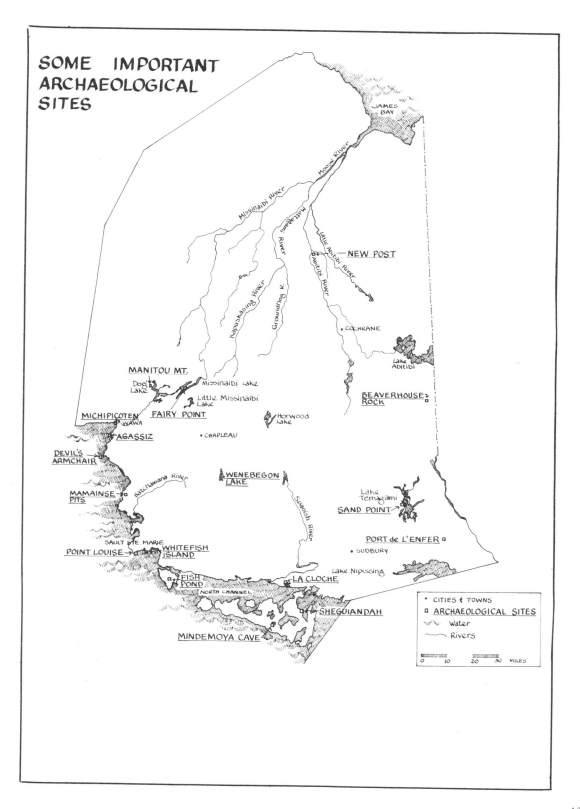

SOME IMPORTANT ARCHAEOLOGICAL SITES

JAMES BAY

Moose River

Missinaibi River

Mattagami River

Little Abitibi River

NEW POST

Abitibi River

Kapuskasing River

Groundhog R.

• COCHRANE

Lake Abitibi

MANITOU MT.

Dog Lake

Missinaibi Lake

Little Missinaibi Lake

FAIRY POINT

Horwood Lake

BEAVERHOUSE ROCK

MICHIPICOTEN

•WAWA

AGASSIZ

• CHAPLEAU

DEVIL'S ARMCHAIR

WENEBEGON LAKE

Batchawana River

Lake Temagami

MAMAINSE PITS

Spanish River

SAND POINT

PORT de L'ENFER

SAULT STE. MARIE

• SUDBURY

POINT LOUISE

WHITEFISH ISLAND

FISH POND

Lake Nipissing

LA CLOCHE

NORTH CHANNEL

SHEGUIANDAH

MINDEMOYA CAVE

• CITIES & TOWNS
▫ ARCHAEOLOGICAL SITES
〰 Water
⌇ Rivers

0   10   20   30   MILES

43

The different styles of decoration on these pot sherds from Whitefish Island represent 1,500 years of ceramic production.

THE MICHIPICOTEN SITE – A STRATIFIED OJIBWA VILLAGE NEAR WAWA

Few sites have been investigated for as long and as frequently as the large, stratified, Indian village situated at the mouth of the Michipicoten River. It was first noted before the turn of the twentieth century and is rediscovered almost yearly, for erosion continually exposes artifacts along the riverbank.

Michipicoten is a deeply buried site. Its lowest levels of occupation lie under a mantle of sand higher than a tall man. Bare dunes in front of the site are continuously swept by Lake Superior's winds and the blown sand has subsequently buried each occupation.

Sites like Michipicoten and Whitefish Island are the largest Indian villages in northeastern Ontario. They served as the long-term, heartland centres for families. At Michipicoten, archaeologists have traced the development of Ojibwa material culture through the last eight centuries of the prehistoric era and well into historic times.

Tools of a different trade. Dust pans and masons' trowels are commonly used when scraping back the layers of time.

BEAVERHOUSE ROCK – A SITE OF LEGEND NEAR KIRKLAND LAKE

Totally different sites are found at various remote localities across the region. Beaverhouse Rock is the embodiment of an Ojibwa legend about a giant beaver that once roamed the countryside around the Misema River and Beaverhouse Lake. Indeed, the rounded contours of the massive granite exposure of Beaverhouse Rock do resemble the outline of a beaver.

Like most folkscape sites, Beaverhouse Rock is part of a larger complex of ceremonial sites. A set of faint pictographs occurs across the channel from Beaverhouse Rock, and an aged Indian informant tells of an unmarked sacred offering spot that is located nearby.

FISH POND SITE, ST JOSEPH ISLAND

St. Joseph is a large, thirty-mile-wide island located where the St. Mary's River enters Lake Huron. Far off in the interior of this terraced and forested island, we found a small prehistoric Indian campsite that we named the Fish Pond Site.

Local people refer to the area as "the ponds in the mountain". It is a very special location. Steep sand dunes form a ring around a group of spring-fed ponds and small streams. The area is reminiscent of Michigan or southern Ontario. The actual site lies at the point where the ponds become the small, undistinguished stream that drains them. Such a specific ecological setting attracted prehistoric hunters and their families because of the waterfowl and game that it offered them.

As an archaeological entity, the site typifies the small, but important, seasonal camps once used by Indian families. We found a few triangular arrowheads, some scrapers and flint blade knives, part of an Indian pipe, one decorated cooking pot, and a native copper tool. These and a few other artifacts lay scattered in the sand around a stone-lined hearth.

Even today, after years of land-clearing and intensive hunting, the area still supports abundant wildlife. It takes little imagination to reconstruct the scene portrayed by the archaeological finds. As I sat for a while, surrounded by waist-high ferns and soft sand, dozens of native trout, a red fox, ducks, and a blue heron came into view from my vantage point on the high dunes. I could almost hear the birch bark being fitted onto lodge poles and smell a roast cooking slowly over the hearth that we had just recorded.

SAND POINT – A TEMPORARY CAMPSITE ON LAKE TEMAGAMI

A low sandy spit, projecting from the west side of Lake Temagami, holds the remains of a series of temporary Indian camps. Like hundreds of similar sites in the region, Sand Point represents an area often used by Indian hunters and travellers.

Small sites can be as informative as larger settlements in the reconstruction of past lifeways. Our salvage dig at Sand Point revealed evidence of trade connections from two different time periods.

Prehistoric Indians of the Temagami region used the site at some time around the fifteenth century A.D. As we excavated a large, stone-lined hearth, we found ample evidence of their stone tools and broken cooking pots. Two items stood out as trade or outside objects. One arrowhead was flaked in a style not found locally. After identification in the regional archaeological laboratory, it proved to be a typical Neutral Indian arrowpoint. The Neutral Indians lived in the area of southern Ontario from Hamilton through the Niagara Peninsula. The type of flint also helped to verify this connection, since it was Onondaga chert that occurs in the Neutral homeland along the shores of Lake Erie. A smashed Iroquois clay pot was also found at the Sand Point site. It too once travelled to this site with an Indian trader.

A later occupational deposit at Sand Point contained a silver ornament. This pierced silver heart probably broke off of a local Indian's clothing sometime around 1810. It is likely that local furs were exchanged for such silver goods. Some people might interpret this as the first archaeological evidence of a broken heart.

An arrowhead, some pot sherds, and a small piece of silver are scant evidence, yet each item helps to open the doors of time for a look into the past.

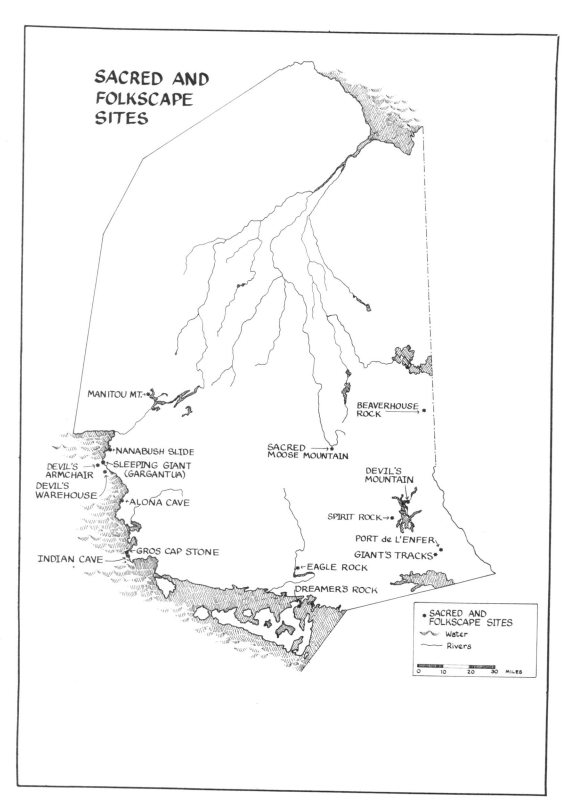

SACRED AND
FOLKSCAPE
SITES

MANITOU MT.

BEAVERHOUSE
ROCK

NANABUSH SLIDE
DEVIL'S → SLEEPING GIANT
ARMCHAIR (GARGANTUA)
DEVIL'S
WAREHOUSE
ALONA CAVE

SACRED →
MOOSE MOUNTAIN

DEVIL'S
MOUNTAIN

SPIRIT ROCK →

PORT de L'ENFER
GIANT'S TRACKS

INDIAN CAVE GROS CAP STONE

EAGLE ROCK

DREAMER'S ROCK

SACRED AND
FOLKSCAPE SITES
Water
Rivers

0   10   20   30   MILES

47

The unmistakeable pierced rock that is known as the Devil's Armchair.

PORTE DE L'ENFER — AN ANCIENT OCHRE MINE NEAR MATTAWA

Red ochre played an important role in the ceremonial life of northern Indians. Ochre was used to paint pictographs, to decorate the skin of the living and deceased, and often to be smeared on ritualistic artifacts.

On the Mattawa River, there is an unnatural opening in the rock walls that has been noted by travellers ever since the earliest explorers. Voyageurs called it Porte de L'Enfer, literally "the gates of hell". Their name for this ancient ochre mine probably reflected Indian legends of the era. Such sites usually harbour a guardian spirit.

When archaeologists examined Porte de L'Enfer, they found evidence of considerable quarrying of ochre veins. A workshop for the removal of the ochre from its rock matrix was found above the mine.

Only one other ochre mine, on an island in Lake Superior, is known in Ontario.

DEVIL'S ARMCHAIR — A VOTIVE SITE ON LAKE SUPERIOR

A strange, sawtoothed rock juts above the waterline near Cape Gargantua on Lake Superior.

Local Indians and fishermen call it the Devil's Armchair, for the rock's deeply imprinted surface seems to have been sat upon by a giant. Ojibwa mythology considers this site to be the work of the trickster hero, Nanabush, a giant who roamed the landscape years ago.

Aside from being a focus of north shore legends, the Devil's Armchair site serves as a place for offerings. Early explorers, like Alexander Henry, wrote about the local custom of leaving tobacco, cloth, and other offerings on the rock to ensure safe travel on the often stormy waters of Lake Superior.

Old traditions linger on, as I found when I first visited the north shore. While interviewing people in the little coastal communities for information on historic places, I found that the fishermen always would refer to the Devil's Armchair. Many told me that local fish-boats stopped at the rock to fling a cigarette or a coin to "the old man, the devil, they say". The practice continues strongly today after a documented history of several hundred years. Even non-Indian fishermen have adopted the custom.

MANITOU MOUNTAIN – A SACRED MOUNTAIN ON DOG LAKE

An Indian guide couldn't solve the mystery of Manitou Mountain for me. He only added to the legendary aura of the place when he said, "I don't know much about it, but the old people always feared the spirits that live there. They used to do their magic up there, those medicine people. But that's a long time ago".

Sacred mountains occur sporadically throughout the north, but their identity is being lost as the old traditions fade away. These sites probably were used in ancient times for shamanistic rituals, burial, and secret ceremonies.

MAMAINSE PITS – COPPER SOURCES ON LAKE SUPERIOR

The only known prehistoric copper quarries in Ontario can be found on the eastern shore of Lake Superior near Mamainse Harbour. These pits are filled with the rubble left from copper extraction. Battered stone hammers left by the Indians who once worked the copper deposits also lie in the depressions. Copper from Mamainse, as well as from the more extensive sources in the upper peninsula of Michigan, was used for thousands of years throughout Ontario and the neighbouring American states.

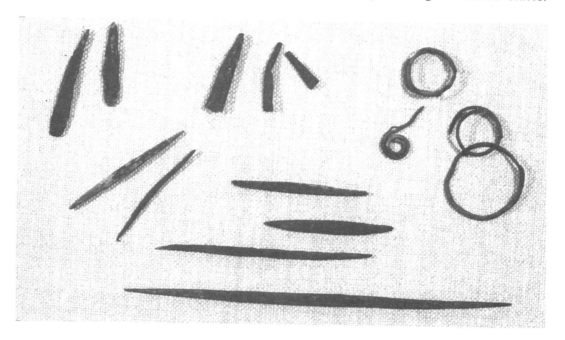

The long, sharp native copper objects are awls or leather punches. Indians also made beads and other ornaments out of copper.

FAIRY POINT — A PREHISTORIC ART GALLERY ON MISSINAIBI LAKE

Rock art sites form a large part of the archaeological inventory of northeastern Ontario. Fairy Point with its large numbers of paintings is the most spectacular pictograph site. Groups of strange creatures and symbols extend for a long distance on the cliffs of Missinaibi Lake. Frozen in time, there are caribou, men, dogs, canoes, and abstract glyphs painted by an ancient artist's hand. The raw power of Missinaibi Lake hurls against the towering painted cliffs. Only granite and timeless secret symbols can endure the elemental forces. It will take years of study to record these and other cliff paintings.

NEW POST — A REMOTE FUR POST ON THE ABITIBI RIVER

Some archaeological sites are only a footnote in the heritage story. Hudson's Bay Company New Post, situated on the Abitibi River halfway between Cochrane and Moosonee, represents a small nineteenth-century settlement that never achieved much prominence or importance. Today, the site serves as a time capsule of Canadian history in the James Bay Lowland area.

As we first approached the New Post site, several years ago, we observed a striking example of erosion and site destruction. The waters of the Abitibi River, with levels raised artificially by hydro-electric generating stations, have washed away much of the site. The foundation of a building shown fifty feet away from the water in an 1890's photograph now lies cut in half on the present riverbank.

People tend to regard archaeological sites located deep in the boreal forest as being safe from disturbance. Unfortunately nature, resource development, and recreational activities often cause considerable archaeological site disturbance, even in the most isolated reaches of the region.

Besides being a fur trader's settlement, the New Post site holds rare evidence of historic Indian campgrounds. Very few old Indian sites are recorded in the vast forest north of the height of land.

A fur trader's cemetery lies hidden in the forest behind New Post. There we photographed rare ornate wooden grave markers and the lichen-covered headstones of long forgotten families. The silence and isolation of the site create a feeling of stepping into the past, when Canada was a young nation and men sought fur and adventure.

LA CLOCHE POST — A REGIONALLY IMPORTANT SITE NEAR ESPANOLA

While New Post represents a secondary outpost of fur trade commerce, the series of fur posts at La Cloche show the development that took place at a major fur trade centre. Today, a few stone walls and other ruins can be seen scattered across the fields and forest of the La Cloche provincial park reserve. It took four years of archaeological exploration to locate the remains of over thirty fur trade buildings, including such structures as the factor's house, the labourer's quarters, a barn, root cellars, and an independent fur trader's cabins.

Our excavations uncovered not only thousands of items from the nineteenth-century, but we also unexpectedly discovered two Indian villages. One of these Indian sites is nearly two thousand years old.

Favoured camping spots on well-travelled waterways proved attractive for settlement and trade throughout the prehistoric and the historic eras. La Cloche is such a place. It gains its regional significance from the diversity of occupations represented there and the wealth of information on past life-ways that it contains. A real bonus in archaeology comes at sites like La Cloche. After finishing excavation of the floor of a voyageur's cabin, we could continue down another level into a buried woodland Indian fishing station.

A peaceful scene at La Cloche.

SHEGUIANDAH — A PREHISTORIC WORKSHOP AND QUARRY ON MANITOULIN ISLAND

Its not unusual to walk across a forest floor littered with broken rocks. At one such location on Manitoulin Island, the rocks are more than rocks, for the hundreds of thousands of quartzite pieces underfoot were all worked by ancient man.

Quarry sites can be found throughout the Great Lakes area. The Indians did not overlook many outcrops of stone with superior flaking qualities that could be utilized. The hunters of long ago made lance tips, arrowheads, and knives from a wide variety of flints (also called cherts), quartzites, rhyolite, and even agates.

The Sheguiandah site on Manitoulin Island was a popular source for a fine-grained white quartzite. Its use began over ten thousand years ago, and continued at least to the second century A.D. Debris from the quarrying-out of suitable quartzite covers several acres of the site. Digs have shown that the Indians worked down several feet into the solid rock for their favourite raw material. Like any stone tool source spot, hundreds of waste fragments remain for every tool taken away.

PIKE ISLAND, WENEBEGON LAKE — AN UNUSUAL PREHISTORIC SITE NEAR CHAPLEAU

In 1979, we discovered an important prehistoric campsite on Wenebegon Lake in the Chapleau district. At first, the Pike Island site on Wenebegon Lake appeared to be a typical Indian camping spot with the usual assortment of artifacts.

The site was carefully mapped and excavated using mason's trowels, screens, and other archaeological tools to remove the thin layer of soil. The dig was important for two reasons. Firstly, the Pike Island site was being destroyed through recent human activity. A commercial fly-in fishing operation had illegally used this island as a regular commercial campsite. The combined effects of rooting stones out for fire circles, foot traffic, garbage and latrine pits, and stripped vegetation caused the mantle of soil to erode and wash into the lake. In a few more years there would not have been an archaeological site to find, only a bare dome of rock. The 1979 dig concentrated on areas most affected by modern use, and we estimate that half of the site was salvaged.

The second reason for the dig's importance only came to light during the past winter as we studied the artifacts and wrote up a report of Pike Island.

During the field work, we unearthed the standard assortment of Indian artifacts that survive the highly acidic soils of the Canadian Shield forest: bits of broken cooking pots, numerous flint flakes left from making stone tools, a couple of arrowheads, and fragments of ancient Indian pipes.

While writing up the analysis of the artifacts, I was stumped in a search for an arrowhead comparable to the long, off-white point found at Pike Island. I turned the stone over and over trying without success to remember similar examples from northeastern Ontario.

The time-worn saying, "when in doubt, ask", proved to be fruitful. I mailed the Pike Island arrowhead to other archaeologists until one identified the stone tool as Rama quartzite. The nearest outcrops of this stone are in western Quebec near James Bay.

Western Quebec is a long way from Chapleau district and how a tool flaked from Rama quartzite ended up on Wenebegon Lake remains a mystery. Did some Cree hunter wander south deep into Ojibwa territory hundreds of years ago? Until we conduct further archaeological work in the height-of-land zone, we will not know whether the artifact represents a chance occurrence or regular trade and visits between distant areas.

The well-travelled arrowhead from Pike Island.

There is another mystery at Wenebegon Lake. As we washed and catalogued the pieces of fired clay vessels, we discovered that the decorated sherds represented more than the standard Indian cooking pots. Many of the small sherds were portions of prehistoric pipes. Such pipes, which were used in ceremonies and rituals, are rare finds in northern Ontario. By carefully studying the decorative motifs, we separated six pipes from the handful of pottery. This high incidence of ceremonial objects at such an obscure site is also difficult to explain at present.

Was Pike Island more than a seasonal fishing site? Perhaps a conjurer's island, used for secret rites? We don't know now, but we plan to salvage the remainder of the site.

The discoveries made at Pike Island demonstrate the importance of rescue archaeology. Any unassessed site, including a seemingly common site like this, holds great potential and merits attention. Archaeologists, like many tellers of fishing stories, tend to concentrate on the "big ones". What else are we missing? I think that the tiny Pike Island site may surprise us again.

THE AGASSIZ SITE — A PUCKASAW PIT SITE ON LAKE SUPERIOR

A mysterious group of sites with man-made pits, low stone walls, and stone rings are found on some cobble beaches of Lake Superior and Lake Huron. These are often called puckasaw pit sites, since the first discoveries were made near the Puckasaw River on Lake Superior. Cobble beaches look like normal sand beaches, with one exception. Instead of being composed of sand grains, cobble beaches are an accumulation of egg- to melon-sized round rocks. Groups of prehistoric Indians often dug into the cobbles to make various sized pits. Sometimes, as the artist's representation of the Agassiz site shows, the depressions have dry stone walls around their perimeter.

The Agassiz site, located near Old Woman Bay in Lake Superior Provincial Park, represents a typical complex puckasaw pit site. It is one of several dozen such ancient ruins on Lake Superior. The lower elevations of the beach are dotted with man-made pits several feet deep, while the largest pit and other stone alignments occur in the upper beach.

Digs at puckasaw pit sites are frustrating for their lack of artifacts. Most items ever lost on a cobble beach percolate down through the rocks, dropping deeply down beyond retrieval. As a test, I once threw a handful of pennies onto a small area of cobble beach. Then I tried to excavate the spot by removing rocks. I ended wiser for the knowledge about such sites, and poorer for the loss of coins. I only found three cents.

Elsewhere archaeologists have found a few flint flakes, pot sherds, and animal bones in and around the pits. Interpretation is not possible based on the low numbers of artifacts, but the altered rock features do have ethnographic counterparts in Ojibwa tradition. We believe that the structures with rectangular walls at these sites are remnants of Grand Medicine Society lodges. Perhaps the nearby pits served as vision quest spots. As is often the story in archaeology, there are more questions than answers for these sites.

This puckasaw pit is surrounded by a wall of cobbles. Such structures are often called "thunderbird nests" by Indians.

MINDEMOYA CAVE – AN OTTAWA BURIAL CAVE ON MANITOULIN ISLAND

In 1888, a group of duck hunters discovered a long forgotten Indian burial cave on Manitoulin Island. The cave was found in a limestone escarpment on the shore of Lake Mindemoya. Piles of human bones lay on its ledges and floor.

The cave is high enough to walk into upright and it is over fifty feet deep. Indian burial caves occur only in the Lake Huron basin. Only a few widely scattered examples are known. When true caves were not available, the ancient tribes used low rocky ledges and recesses on offshore islands. The nineteenth-century discoverers of the Mindemoya cave didn't share the respect for burial sites that we do today. Their unbound-ed enthusiasm caused them to carry away the bundles of skulls and long bones that filled this natural and secret burial crypt. A few artifacts such as arrowheads and a drilled clamshell ornament were found with the piles of bones.

Since the practice of using open, rather than buried, cemeteries was restricted to the Lake Huron area, archaeologists suspect that these sites were used by the ancestors of the Ottawa. Comparable sites have been recorded elsewhere on Manitoulin Island, near Tobermory on the Bruce Peninsula, and in the straits of Mackinac.

Archaeology and northerners

Visitors to our widely scattered digs come loaded with questions like "What are you finding? How old are the artifacts? Why dig here?".

Working in archaeology is a quick method of meeting northerners. Digs, site surveys, and general bush work bring us in contact with Indians, trappers, farmers, young foresters, construction workers, fishermen, and other fellow residents of the Canadian Shield country. Everyone seems to be seeking the peculiar northern identity that is an amalgamation of our collective past, our geographic location, and a rapidly changing landscape.

Its always surprising to find people who are strangers in their own land, but this often happens in northern Ontario. Few residents have any concept of the eight to ten thousand years of prehistory that forms our collective heritage. Even the broader outlines of the last three hundred years are only vaguely comprehended.

Having talked to hundreds of people throughout northeastern Ontario in the past eight years, we realize how keen the public is to learn about its archaeological heritage. The story from the past is oftentimes romantic and adventuresome, but its true merit lies in the lessons we gather about relationships between people, resources, and the environment.

The true magic of archaeology is found in the interpretation of the finds. Whenever an archaeologist travels back in time, he takes the public along to an unknown world. Our ancestors first explored this continent as voyageurs, native hunters and fishermen, immigrants, and merchants. The excitement of such discovery can still be enjoyed through an acquaintance with our past. The search goes on.

Indian guides once shot Whitefish rapids with canoes full of tourists.

The author is shown making direct reproductions of Indian rock paintings at Agawa Bay on Lake Superior.